DISCOVER SERIES
PESCADO

Angelote

Róbalo

Pez Verde Asiático Betta

Atún Azul

Angelote de Cara Azul

Carpa

Pez Payaso

Dorado

Huevos de Pezcado

Lenguado

Pez Disco de Oro

Pez de Colores

Guppy

Lamprea

Pulpo

Medusa Rosada

Caballo de Mar

Camarón

Rodaballo Solo

Pulpo Chico

Pez Globo Espinoso

Calamar

Estrella de Mar

Titanista

Espiga Amarilla

Make Sure to Check Out the Other Discover Series Books from Xist Publishing:

Published in the United States by Xist Publishing
www.xistpublishing.com
PO Box 61593 Irvine, CA 92602

© 2018 by Xist Publishing All rights reserved
Translated by Victor Santana
No portion of this book may be reproduced without express permission of the publisher
All images licensed from Fotolia
First Spanish Edition

ISBN: 978-1-5324-0727-7   eISBN: 978-1-5324-0728-4

xist Publishing

Ingram Content Group UK Ltd.
Milton Keynes UK
UKHW052209110723
424907UK00007B/46